INVENTING THE HAWK

PAPL
DISCARDED

ALSO BY LORNA CROZIER

Inside Is the Sky 1976
Crow's Black Joy 1979
Humans and Other Beasts 1980
No Longer Two People (with Patrick Lane) 1981
The Weather 1983
The Garden Going On Without Us 1985
Angels of Flesh, Angels of Silence 1988

Wapiti regional library

INVENTING
THE HAWK

Lorna Crozier

9403509

M&S

Copyright © 1992 Lorna Crozier

Reprinted 1993

All rights reserved. The use of any part of this
publication reproduced, transmitted in any form or by
any means, electronic, mechanical, photocopying,
recording, or otherwise, or stored in a retrieval system,
without the prior written consent of the publisher – or,
in case of photocopying or other reprographic copying,
a licence from Canadian Reprography Collective – is an
infringement of the copyright law.

CANADIAN CATALOGUING IN PUBLICATION DATA

Crozier, Lorna, 1948–
Inventing the hawk

Poems.
ISBN 0-7710-2477-0

I. Title.

PS8555.R615 1992   C811'.54   C92-093070-0
PR9199.3.C715 1992

The publisher makes grateful acknowledgement to the
Ontario Arts Council for its financial assistance.

Set in Minion at M&S
Printed and bound in Canada on acid-free paper

McClelland & Stewart Inc.
The Canadian Publishers
481 University Avenue
Toronto, Ontario
M5G 2E9

For my mother and brother,
and in memory of my father,
Emerson Crozier, who died in May 1990.

This is the walled city, family. Within,
all the love and hate a body needs.

ALICE DERRY

ACKNOWLEDGEMENTS

I wrote "The New Poem" after reading Charles Wright's poem of the same title. The first line of "A Man and a Woman" is the title of a poem by Robert Bly.

Some of the poems were broadcast on CBC's "Ambience" and "Morningside" and published in *Saturday Night, NeWest Review, Descant, Grain, Canadian Literature, The Malahat Review, Border Crossings, Event, Exile, Quarry, Southern Review, Western Report, Books in Canada, CVII,* and *Prairie Fire.* The sequence "Time to Praise" was commissioned by editor Jerome Martin for a book entitled *Alternative Futures for Prairie Agricultural Communities* (University of Alberta Press, 1991).

Once again, I would like to thank Donna Bennett for her friendship and editing skills, Patrick Lane for his advice and companionship, and CBC radio producer Wayne Schmalz for his continued support of my writing. This book would not have been written without the financial support of the Saskatchewan Arts Council, the Ontario Arts Council, the University of Toronto Writer-in-Residence Program, and the Saskatchewan Writers' Guild Artists'/Writers' Colonies. Finally, I want to thank my mother for allowing me to reveal some old family secrets.

CONTENTS

III.   THE GARDENS WITHIN US

IV.   MOVING TOWARD SPEECH

I

Dictionary of Symbols

In the silence of snow
far from the city lights,
a baker is baking bread
under the stars.

He wears a long white smock,
his hat tall as a loaf
that rose too high.
There is flour
on his face and hands,
flour in his mouth and eyes.

You can't see him
                    for all that white
even if you walk past the houses
into the snowy dark,
into the smells of your childhood.

But he is baking,
pounding and shaping the dough.
On every loaf he pinches a name
with his fingers, his broad thumbs.
It could be your father's name,
your mother's. You never say it
out loud, never feel it
in your mouth. Nothing
is more silent than that name.

While you sleep in your ordinary bed,
under the stars on a snowy plain
a baker is baking bread. Rows of loaves
shaped by his hands are rising,

rising for someone's funeral feast,
rising for that moment when you break
the bread, its good smell
all around you.

The woman who undresses in the dark
with the curtains open. Slowly
she twists her hands around her back,
unhooks her bra, slides her panties
over her hips and down her legs.
No one can see her.
There is more light outside than in her room.
But she stands at the window naked as if
the moon were a mirror held in night's hands.
It is the colour of her breasts
when they are full of milk,
it is dimpled like her thighs,
her tired belly, it waxes and wanes.
She tries to hold it in her arms,
imagines wading into it,
all its roundness one tranquil sea.

On the street below her a man
in a red farmer's cap pulls a rusty wagon
full of empty bottles down the sidewalk,
the wheels rattling. She wants to show him
the moon, its calm indifference
on a summer evening when all her children
are asleep, when her husband kneels on a bed
in another house, entering a woman
from behind, so he can watch himself
disappear into the flesh,
his hands on her buttocks,
round and glistening with sweat.

The woman who undresses in the dark,
stands at the window, turns on the light.

This is what it looks like, she says,
this pale celestial body, faceless
as the moon is faceless, coldly luminescent.
You can stare at it forever
and never burn your eyes.

On the day named for the animals,
the tortoises crawl out of the soup vats
all across France, leaving herb-scented tracks
across the polished floors. Out of the poachers'
bags and through the restaurant windows
the quail fly, land on the linen tablecloths
and gather the speckled eggs to their breasts.
Foxes reclaim their silver coats
from the storage vaults, chew off the buttons
and slip into their smooth cold skins.
The elephants pull on their feet,
reassemble their long luminous tusks
earring by ivory earring, bead by bead.
One by one they claim what is theirs
and vanish
with the Sabre Tooth, the Dodo Bird,
the Dire Wolf. Only the animals
man has tamed or broken
remain, less
beautiful than they once had been,
for all that is wild
has gone out of them, even
the Appaloosa in the bluegrass meadow
eats only the hay thrown over the fence
and will not run.

In the solarium pool
she separates like milk
into what is heavy and what is not,
splits like sunlight
passed through a prism.

On the bottom,
dolphin-grey and graceful
her shadow swims.
Eyes closed,
it knows only one thing,
something she can't articulate
but it has to do with motion.

On the ceiling made of glass
her reflection looks back at her,
not with recognition
but with slight surprise
as her head, arms and legs
form the five points of a star.

In between, the part of her
that feels the warmth of water,
her muscles' stretch and pull,
repeats the strokes
she learned as a child.

She wonders how she'll bring
these parts back together.
If she climbs from the pool
will she become an ordinary woman

with children waiting, her darkness
folded like a scarf and tucked away,
her reflection moving to the bathroom mirror?

She hesitates to swim to the ladder,
feel the steel rungs
press against her soles. Maybe
this is how a woman drowns,
raising her arm three times,
not a call for help
but a gesture of acknowledgement,
of recognition

as she becomes one
with her body,
one with her shadow,
one with her drifting star.

On the first day God said
Let there be light.
And there was light.
On the second day
God said, *Let there be light,*
and there was more light.

What are you doing? asked God's wife,
knowing he was the dreamy sort.
You created light yesterday.

I forgot, God said. *What can I do
about it now?*

*Nothing, said his wife.
But pay attention!*
And in a huff she left
to do the many chores
a wife must do in the vast
though dustless rooms of heaven.

On the third day God said
Let there be light. And
on the fourth and fifth
(his wife off visiting his mother).

When she returned there was only
the sixth day left. The light
was so blinding, so dazzling
God had to stretch and stretch the sky to hold it
and the sky took up all the room –
it was bigger than anything

even God could imagine.
Quick, his wife said,
make something to stand on!
God cried, *Let there be earth!*
and a thin line of soil
nudged against the sky like a run-over snake
bearing all the blue in the world on its back.

On the seventh day God rested
as he always did. Well, *rest*
wasn't exactly the right word,
his wife had to admit.
On the seventh day God
went into his study
and wrote in his journal
in huge curlicues and loops
and large crosses on the *t*'s,
changing all the facts, of course,
even creating Woman
from a Man's rib, imagine that!
But why be upset? she thought.
Who's going to believe it?

Anyway, she had her work to do.
Everything he'd forgotten
she had to create
with only a day left to do it.
Leaf by leaf,
paw by paw, two by two,
and now nothing
could be immortal
as in the original plan.

Go out and multiply, yes,
she'd have to say it,
but there was too little room
for life without end,
forever and ever,
on that thin spit of earth
under that huge prairie sky.

She took the two male turtles
from a friend because his kids
when they grew up
found them ugly, turned away
from their wrinkled necks,
their greed for meat,
the swampy smell they carry
on their skin. She'd love

to set them free, imagines
dropping them like stones into
a frog-filled pond, a turtle paradise,
mud and jellied eggs, water
lilies floating on the light.
But this is not their country

or their time. Even if
they could survive the cold,
the river here's polluted
and any boy
who'd see them basking on the banks
would take them home to a smaller cage
till he outgrew them.

All she can do is give them treats –
bits of steak and bloody sausage,
make sure there are ample rocks
and a growing light that imitates
a kinder sun. In France

Gérard de Nerval tied a lobster to a leash
and led it down Montmartre.

"It makes the perfect pet," he said,
"because it doesn't bark
and knows the secrets of the sea."
The idea of it – the turtles paddling
behind her on cement,
blinking at the polished
quickly moving shells of feet –
can make her weep. Every day

they grow bigger and bigger
in their transparent cage,
a loneliness
that paces back and forth inside her.
When they press against the glass,
gaze at her with cold green eyes
she'd like to know their secrets.

At least there'll be no others
to remind her
when they're gone, no
eggs, no baby turtles
scuttling for some distant
river, lake or pond,
an ancient mating ground.

She watches the soft
muscled ropes of their
black penises unfurl
                         thin and long
moving like separate creatures
through the water.

Tentative and weightless,
they touch the wall of glass
as if they were exploring the
red-eared female's shell
        – there and there and there –
trying to find the one way
out or in.

A fly tapping on the windowpane
makes the same sound
wanting in or out.
Next door a dog barks
behind a sign that says *Beware.*
Beware the season. The light
low to the earth
is pulled to the breaking point.
You too could so easily break,
take to the air in feathers,
or, staying in one place,
swing like a weather vane
in any direction, turn
like a bush into fire.
Your heart, a hummingbird,
rides the backs of wild geese
the way it rides in you
small and unnoticed
in that place behind your ribs,
its ruby throat silent
as *(beware the season)*
the geese bear
the beauty of their burden
farther and farther south.

Of all the body
it's the creature closest to the sea.
Snail-moist, all tuck and salty
muscle, it opens and closes
like a sea anemone. Mute
but several tongued,
minus legs and memory,
it's what moves you
to bowl and basin,
to hollows in the stone
where water gathers after storms.
It draws you past the breakers
to the wild, the open,
gives your arms and naked thighs
their power and pull. More
reptilian than cat, its brain
is the oldest brain, prelapsarian,
soft moss and weeping fern.
Stopped on its evolutionary trail.
Beached, becalmed, stranded without
gills, scales or jewelled tail,
yet you feel it
flex and flutter
beneath your lover's tongue
as feather
after slow inevitable feather
it dreams the world's
first wings.

Breasts are back!
You can see them everywhere.
On movie screens, in restaurants,
at baseball games. You can feel them
bump against you in the subway
like friendly spaniels.
Big as melons they bob
behind grocery carts,
they pout under denim.
Breasts are back!
They won't stay locked up.
They shrink the space
in elevators, they leap
out of jogging bras,
find their own way
down the road, running
hand in hand. They wave
at you from buses,
swaying around corners
and swinging back. Oh,
how they move! Graceful
ballerinas, a *pas de deux.*
They rise and fall
under your grandmother's floral apron,
they flutter under your daughter's
t-shirt, small shy sparrows
learning to fly.
Breasts are back. On the beach
nipples peek from bikinis
as if they were eyes, wide open,
wanting to watch the sea.
Sailors rise from the Atlantic,

clutching their Mae Wests
for breasts are back.

But wait! Not just any breasts.
A breast should not be able to support
a pencil underneath it.
A breast must fit into a champagne glass,
not the beer mug you raise
to your mouth on a hot summer day.
A breast must have nipples
no bigger than a dime.
A breast must be hairless,
not even one or two small hairs
for your lover to remove
with his teeth. A breast must bear
no stretch marks, must be smooth
as alabaster, luminous as pearls.

Enough of that!
Let's stand up for breasts
any size, any colour,
breasts shaped like kiwi fruit,
like mandolins, like pouter pigeons,
breasts playful and shameless as puppies.
Breasts that pop buttons,
breasts with rose tattoos.
Let's give them the vote.
Let's make them mayor for the day.
Let's remember our old secret
loyalties, the first words
they placed in our mouths,
the sweet warm vowels
of our mother's milk

urging us toward our lives
before we even knew our names.
Breasts are back, let's shout it,
and they're here to stay!

You can't get pregnant
if it's your first time.

You can't get pregnant
if you do it standing up,
if you don't French kiss,
if you pretend
you won't let him
but just can't stop.

You can't get pregnant
if you go to the bathroom
right after,
if you ride a horse
bareback, if you jump
up and down on one leg,
if you lie in the snow
till your bum feels numb,
if you do it in the shower,
if you eat garlic,
if you wear a girdle,
if it's only your second time.

You can't get pregnant
if he keeps his socks on,
if he's captain of the football team,
if he says he loves you,
if he comes quickly,
if you don't come at all,
if it's only your third time.

You can't get pregnant
if he tells you
you won't.

The woman from Home Care is late. She apologizes, but she had a helluva day yesterday. She was supposed to go fishing with her boyfriend in LaRonge, packed the sleeping bags in his truck, found the Coleman stove and fishing rods, made a big pot of chili while he was supposed to be at work, poured it into coffee tins, then drove to her friend's to pick up a cooler. This woman's the same age as her mother, but guess what? There he was fishin' already, she says, but in her friend's bed, get my drift? So, she goes back to her place and waits, gets all dressed up as if she's going out, puts on her new shirt and cowboy boots. When he gets there, sits at the kitchen table, all sorry, blubbering *never again,* she takes the boots to him and she means what she says, she kicks him right in the face. Boy did he look stunned, like a big one when the hook bites in, too stunned to lift a finger, blood spattering his shirt. And he deserves it. His first wife said he used to beat on her but who wanted to believe it? *Fishin' good?* she says. Now he's gone, she means for *ever,* but he'll never be rid of her. She opened him right above the cheek – there'll be a scar there three inches long saying *howdee-do* every time he looks in the mirror and he's the kind of guy has to shave twice a day for the rest of his life so that's a lot of lookin'.

At the dinner party the woman
who intends to make love to my husband
tries to give me a recipe.
I have too many now, ones
I've saved for years from magazines
as if they're messages
of love or wisdom
that will teach me how to live.

They spill from drawers,
from the pockets of my bathrobe,
the pages of my books. Still
she persists, reciting
the ingredients: smoked salmon,
a cup of cream, lemon,
green onions, garlic, and basil.
You'll love it, she says,
and don't hold back –
it's the spices
that make all the difference.

Later when we're home
exchanging stories about the party
before we go to bed,
he says her name out loud,
three times
in the course of conversation
as if he likes the sound of it,
as if he savours each
creamy vowel, each piquant
consonant on his tongue.

I am brushing my teeth.
I pretend I haven't noticed.
At least, I tell myself,
I'll know if he's been with her –
the smell of garlic
where her fingers sweep across his belly
just below the navel
the oh so delicate taste of
basil on his skin.

1

The brown horse grazing in pastures of sleep
is full of soldiers. Each has his own
corner of darkness, his corner of despair.
The soldiers feel the sway of the horse's belly
as she races night across the meadows.
All of them believe they are in the hold
of a ship that smells of grass and forgetfulness
though they can't understand her hours of stillness,
or the mad sound of flies eating her ears.
Each remembers being pushed through the pale
thighs of his wound away from the field
where he fell though he can't remember
the name of the country or the day or the year.
Sailors now, they have crossed oceans of clouds
to reach this green meadow at the end
of the twentieth century where someone
may unlatch a gate for the horse to enter,
open the door between her ribs and let the light
pick among their bones.

2

The farm girl who rides the horse
after her chores are done
has no idea they are there.

If she did, she would not
squeeze her thighs so tight
around the horse's flanks,
she would not ride so hard.

26

Sometimes she thinks
she hears voices
as she lays her cheek
along the horse's neck,
sometimes she has bad dreams.

Already longing for the city
she is bored with horses,
the feral smell of them
on her hands, along
the inside of her legs.

When she brushes the horse
wipes away the lather,
she does not know
it could be foam
from the sea
churned by drowning

or froth from the mouth
of a dying man.

3

The horse without wings
grazes calmly in the meadow.
She has no need of eternity,
no need of bits or bridles.

What she knows beyond
the good sense of her hooves
no one can tell.

If we call her *ship*
if we call her *nightmare,*
if we call her *history,*
she will not care.

When she wants to
she moves, flicks
at flies with her tail,
curls back her lip
and shows her yellow teeth.

When she wants to
she stands
absolutely still.

Thick as her arms,
all skin and muscle
and hidden bone,
they nuzzle her
like a horse's mouth
feeding from her palm
or bunt her
with their flat, blunt heads
like cats.

Mostly they lie still
as the green
on the underside of ice,
barely breathing,
drugged with cold.

In the spring they'll begin
to stir like water
close to the boiling point.

A change of heart,
a change of skins.

For now
they are tolerant,
insouciant,
as they puff and snore,
their yellow eyes
old as amber. Strange
how she can warm herself
at such cold fires.

In the pause
          between seasons,
between two languages,
she sleeps among snakes,
the smell of her
on every listless tongue.

The afternoon I saw Hemingway
on the beach in Adra. It was February.
He was sitting on a camp stool,
painting three little fishing boats
turned over in the sand to keep them dry,
the nets' giant webs stretched
across the wood to catch
the thousand locusts of the light
that rose from the sea on brilliant wings.
I thought it odd
he looked so gentle and at peace, after
the life he'd led, after his violent death,
a simple Sunday painter in a cloth hat,
his brush filling the canvas with blues and crimson,
not for show, not to attract
the tourists and their easy words of praise,
but for himself,
the fishing boats, the winter sun.

I knew I shouldn't speak to him,
that he was through
with talk, just wanted to follow
the language of the light,
his hands remembering
what they had known before
he was a man, the joyful colours spilling
beyond the lines, beyond the form
of things.

I had just arrived in Adra
to spend two months with a friend.
No one answered when I found her house,

knocked on the door,
but I saw her coming down the street toward me,
a thin middle-aged woman walking into
the glare of white-washed walls,
a bag of oranges in one hand.
With the other, she covered her mouth,
not wanting anyone to see
the bruised and broken lip
where her husband had punched her with his fist.

The look on her face when she saw me waiting
was like the one on Hemingway's, not as I'd
just seen him on the beach but in that famous
photograph by Karsh. I'd read about it
in a magazine, Karsh saying
just before he took the picture,
Hemingway's face was wet with tears.
He was in terrible pain
and he apologized – it was after
the safari when his plane had crashed
and he wore a wood support across his back.

All that week I listened to my friend
in the bar of the expatriates' hotel,
then watched her every evening climb the hill
to her husband's house
where some nights she was loved and others
beaten black and blue. Nothing I said made sense
to her. I did not tell her whom I'd seen
painting on the beach my first day there

or mention how her face
made me think of the photograph,
the shyness, the apology, the awkward pain.

We never spoke of Adra
when we met again in Canada.
In fact, we were no longer friends –
I knew what she wanted no one else to know.

If I could speak to her about that time,
I'd tell her now of Hemingway,
of the plain wooden stool
he sat upon,
his hands moving with such
calm and gentle grace
as if they'd known
only brush and paint
and never held a gun.

I'd tell her of the fishing boats,
of the wide-brimmed hat
he wore low upon his head
(his back so straight),
his broad face
stained with tears and shadow.

THE BRAIN

> The brain itself in its skull/Is very cold,
> According to/Albertus Magnus.
> CHARLES SIMIC, "Harsh Climate"

Birds that live among the brain's ice floes
must grow feathers on their feet and eyelids,
all the mammals a density of hair
and layers and layers of fat.

It is no place for reptiles,
their feet that look like human hands,
delicate and hairless,
their fickle skin
changing colour as they move
from stone to flower. In the brain
there is only one colour.

But that can't be true, she says.
In my brain a two-headed skink laps milk
with its blue tongues,
and parrots in their clown jackets
juggle nuts and berries in a jungle
full of insects big as birds.

Albertus Magnus looks across the pillows
at his mistress sitting upright in their bed,
leaning toward him, her hair undone,
then looks past her out the window
at the dark garden, the small
modest flowers invisible though he knows
she planted them while he sat in his study,
entering in his notebook
what often seem, even to him,

unavoidable and terrible discoveries,
written in the smooth perfect longhand
he learned in school.

Should he tell her memory resides
in other places than the brain?
The skink curls inside her warm, humid bowels,
the parrots occupy several many-sided
cells in her liver, and he, himself,
is shipwrecked in her pancreas,
on one small island.

Yes, he says out loud, your brain is warmer
than most others. In the centre of its long
expanse of ice, a fire glows like light
trapped in crystal. That's where you live
most of the time, a small figure wrapped
in furs, the flames telling you
your childhood stories, warming your hands
that smell of mint and lavender
and all around you is the sound
of water running, and one cricket
singing to the huge night.

As she lies back down in bed,
curling her body around his cold limbs,
her hair draped across his shoulder
like the pelt of a mole,
he gives her several names to call
the cricket, translations from the Japanese,
Cricket in the Snowy Tree, Grass Lark,
Little Bell of the Bamboo Grove.

The beautiful blue of ink, ah,
if she could give him that,
place the colour on his lips and tongue.
When he kissed her breasts the words
would write themselves along
the milky white between her veins.

Is it vain to want to be a book
for him? Or more than that, a trilogy,
holy, holy, holy her body writes
on every page marked by his thumbs,
the spittle he licks his fingers with
as he turns deeper into the story, the forest,
the field blue with moonlight
where a woman bends to gather grain,
the landlord and his workers gone.

Not an illuminated manuscript filigreed
by a small monk who warms his hands
over a candle-flame. But a plain book
that might have lain on the floor
near a child's bed
or fit into the trouser pocket of a man
who breaks for lunch,
pages stained by his fingers
greasy from the butter on his bread,
when the whistle blows, his place
marked with the torn cover of a matchbook.

It would be a simple tale
but one that would not fail to hold him,
the word *hearth* repeated several times
and *clavichord* and *bearded wheat* and *drum.*

Every word would be written in hand-
ground India ink, some on her skin and some
in the air around her, moving forward
like an indigo train toward an end,
a destination, a station stop. There
on the final page, in the patient telling
of her body is a sign that spells
home for him. The familiar name –
wherever he has gone –
that will take him in.

When I met you it was as if
I was living in a house by the sea.
Waves sprayed the windows,
slapped the wooden steps.
Yet I opened the door
and a white horse stood there.
He walked through the rooms,
swinging his head from side to side,
his hooves leaving half moons
of sand on the floor.

Make what you will of this. This was
the most natural thing I've ever done,
opening the door, moving aside
for the horse to come in.

Not that you were he. He was simply
a horse, nothing more,
the gentle kind that pulls a wagon
or drags seaweed from the shore,
ankles feathered, great hooves wide as platters.

He wasn't you,
that didn't matter. He looked at me
and we knew each other. That night
I wanted to live. I wanted
to live in a house where the door
swings on hinges smooth as the sea
and a white horse stands,
waiting for a sign.

Come in, I said.

And that was the start of it,
the horse, the light, the electric air.
Somewhere you were walking toward me,
the door to my life swinging open,
the sea, the sea and its riderless horse
waiting to come in.

I have no children and he has five,
three of them grown up, two with their mother.
It didn't matter when I was thirty and we met.
There'll be no children, he said, the first night
we slept together and I didn't care,
thought we wouldn't last anyway,
those terrible fights,
he and I struggling to be the first
to pack, the first one out the door.
Once I made it to the car before him,
locked him out. He jumped on the hood,
then kicked the headlights in.
Our friends said we'd kill each other
before the year was through.

Now it's ten years later.
Neither of us wants to leave.
We are at home with one another,
we are each other's home,
the voice in the doorway,
calling *Come in, come in,*
it's growing dark.

Still, I'm often asked if I have children.

Sometimes I answer yes.
Sometimes we have so much
we make another person.
I can feel her in the night
slip between us, tell my dreams

how she spent her day. *Good night,*
she says, *good night, little mother,*
and leaves before I waken.
Across the lawns she dances
in her white, white dress,
her dream hair flying.

Amanuensis of the gods,
the magpie with his tail
scrawls the messages they want to leave
as they vanish from the world.

Across the blue of flax he writes
the equanimity of bones,
across the yard, between house and barn,
the optic ocean. Scholars from the university,
rabbis and monks arrive with heavy tomes
of explication, computer codes and charts.
As they set up their tents underneath
the power lines the magpie drags his tail,
interstices of sorrow. This must be
one of the greater gods,
they all agree, He is so cryptic.

In heaven a sparrow
walks across the breadboard on tiny feet.
In the flour her tracks say *custard,*
biscuit, goat's milk. The god
who'd rather spend time in the kitchen
than on his parapet of clouds
thinks this is a grocery list
his wife has left for him.
He sends a seraph to find each item,
though he knows there's nothing here
with cloven hooves or mad gold eyes.

Tomorrow, he thinks, I'll tell
Magpie these words.
They can fill a head with wonder.

So full of import and such sweet intent,
a whole life unfolding
in the sounds they make.

Take the first word
custard.

Who baked it?
he must ask his wife.
Who ate it?
Was it good?

She didn't believe the words
when she first heard them, that blue
bodiless sound entering her ear.
But now something was in the air,
a sense of waiting as if
the hawk itself were there
just beyond the light, blinded
by a fine-stitched leather hood
she must take apart with her fingers.
Already she had its voice,
the scream that rose from her belly
echoed in the dark inverted
canyon of her skull.

She built its wings, feather by feather,
the russet smoothness of its head,
the bead-bright eyes,
in that moment between sleep and waking.

Was she the only one
who could remember them,
who knew their shape and colours, the way
they could tilt the world with a list of wings?
Perhaps it was her reason for living
so long in this hard place
of wind and sky, the stunted trees
reciting their litany of loss
outside her window.

Elsewhere surely someone was drawing
gophers and mice out of the air.
Maybe that was also her job,

so clearly she could see them.
She'd have to lie here forever,
dreaming hair after hair,
summoning the paws (her own heart
turning timid, her nostrils twitching).

Then she would cause the seeds
in their endless variety – the ones
floating light as breath,
the ones with burrs and spears
that caught in her socks
when she was a child,
the radiant, uninvented blades of grass.

At night the houses move closer.
They slide together as if the earth
tilts when the sun disappears. Now
there is nothing
between them. Windows
hang like pictures on a gallery wall,
rooms caught for a moment in the light,
and in one, a woman's face,
a portrait someone painted long ago.
The man who walks the street
wants to reach through the pane
with a brush, add a detail here and there.
On the table a bowl of golden pears. *Comice,*
he would call them, loving the word
though he doesn't know what it means.
Behind the figure, he'd stroke the lushness
of a velvet drape, a dog from Velasquez
sleeping on a tasselled pillow. Not this
starkness, this woman's face drawn and drawn again
by the bare bulb hanging from the ceiling.
Like a woman in front of a mirror
she stands at the window, not seeing
beyond the sadness of her face.
If he could, he'd place his image
in a white smock beside her in the glass
and she would be his model. *Triste,*
he must have said, *Dolore, dolore,*
and she took this pose. Soon she will
shrug her shoulders, shake away
the pain and walk from the window
to a room he cannot see. Then

he will put away his brushes,
find an all-night diner where
he won't have to be alone.
He sees himself already there,
waiting for someone
to ask him what he wants,
while in the street the houses
slowly shift their weight
and separate,
just before morning.

II

That Rare, Random Descent

The wait's begun again,
The long wait for the angel,
For that rare, random descent.

SYLVIA PLATH

The honeycomb
that is the mind
storing things

crammed with sweetness,
eggs about to hatch –
the slow thoughts

growing wings and legs,
humming memory's
five seasons, dancing

in the brain's blue light,
each turn and tumble
full of consequence,

distance and desire.
Dangerous to disturb
this hive, inventing clover.

How the mind wants
to be free of you,
move with the swarm,

ascend in the shape
of a blossoming tree –
your head on the pillow

emptied of scent and colour,
winter's cold indifference
moving in.

It thinks the world
into being
with its huge mind,
its pure intelligence.

On the curve
of its crystal
skull
you see yourself,
you see your shadow.

One of you
will put on shoes,
will walk into the world.

The wheat ripples in the wind
like muscles under the skin
of a great cat.

Never have the fields
been so beautiful, so dangerous.
The beards of wheat flick back and forth,
even when the air is still.

In the long dry heat everything awaits
the gazelle-footed touch of the rain.

The horse has been standing
so long in the snow,
the side facing the wind
is white, the other,
black.

The white horse
walks off with the wind.

The black doesn't know
it is only

an absence
cut out of snow.

Now anything could walk
right through it
and disappear.

Most are dead
before they are

completely open
but this one

unfurls every petal
its flawless white

consumes the air
death's own flower

infused with light
allowing us to see

the invisible
unfolding of our days

No one is more white
than she, more melancholy.

You think she is looking at you?

She is looking at no one

You think she feels your skin
as moonlight falls across your shoulders?

She feels nothing.

You think she wants to come down,
nest in that tree with the sleepwalking owls,
rest on your window sill?

She wants nothing.

In the nave of the sky
she's a bouquet of calla lilies,
blooming for the funeral of the world.

That feeling you get,
that shift in the light
is her shadow
               passing over the earth.
Everything else pauses
for one
       heartbeat –
even the birds, even
the cat with wings in his mouth,
even the sisyphus wind.

In heaven
the season for mathematics
is winter. Chalk falls
from the blackboards,
covers the earth.

The angel who invented
arithmetic
is trying to get rid of zero.

She erases and erases
the boards
then starts again

assigning to the numbers
already in the air
their own lost stars
to live on,
their own dark infinity
to name.

Consider the angel of salamanders.

Would it have four legs
and a tail?
Would it play the harp
with slim green fingers,
would it sing and sing?

Once I saw a salamander
in the root cellar, my mother
stabbed it
with a butcher knife,
opened the furnace door
and threw it in. Its back
grew fiery wings.

It flew through my bedroom
when my mother turned off the light,
though I kept my eyes
closed tight
I could feel its flames
sweep just above my hair.

All the colours of my dreams
come from that small angel.

The angels lie down
in the field. That delicate
rustling is not the wind
playing the thin pipes of wheat,
but the angels' feathers,
their dead wings.

You can't see them,
but listen
when you check your crops,
the wheat so golden
it seems to float above the ground.

What a beautiful
sad sound they make,
all those feathers
remembering the wind.

In the half-light of closets
you can still see
lust in the trousers,

the bottom of the legs
caressing dust,
drawing from memory

a pair of shoes, perhaps
the black ones he wore
on his journey through the earth.

In the pocket, the last
grocery list you gave him,
a pencilled check

beside each item. That day
he found everything
and brought it home.

Their marvellous mouths say nothing,
say nothing. What you hear is
their silence. It falls through the seven
celestial spheres, gathers in the dark
behind the rock they rolled from the tomb.
Here their wings translate the air.
Their feet, more beautiful than any Homer knew,
interpret each blade of grass,
an exegesis of the earth. Words,
thoughts, senses are all one body,
the body before you that burns.
All flesh these
words, these extravagant mouths,
mute as swans.

Miraculous and violent
it cruises the air,
its long tail
shimmering
with reptilian light.
The colour blue
gives to fire,
it ignites the hairs
on your arm
and settles there.

Amoral,
atavistic, its gaze
comes from a great height.

It looks at you
as if it knows
exactly
who you are.

III

The Gardens Within Us

There are no gardens save those we carry within us.
OCTAVIO PAZ

A single row of Swiss chard
the only green in the garden,
its plumed leaves a postscript
from a summer gone. The firebugs
we never see outside
move from the cold,
squeeze their flat bodies
under the weather stripping,
through the cracks. One crawls
across the arm of my chair, carries
on its back its hieroglyph of flame.

Two months into fall, my father's
cancer blooming in his veins.
Now the only blossoms are inside.
Ice-poppy, columbine, wild rose.
They send their seeds
down the rivers of my father's blood,
land and put out roots,
push their hard buds
against his skin. His garden
growing in the soft light
his body makes.

                    Late October,
the season dying, inside
our house the firebugs
burning in their own small flames.

Dad, a little drunk, every summer Sunday
brought home a pail of perch
late in the evening like a prize (small,
but the tastiest fish you'll ever eat)
as another man might bring
a box of chocolates or
a rose.

Mom, who had spent the day alone
with me, sat on the back step,
mad as she could be
and gutted them, scraped
the scales with a coke cap
nailed to a stick (he said
he didn't know how to clean them right,
he'd lose the meat and keep
the bones).
I swore I'd not do that
for anyone.

Mom's hands became more fish
than flesh,
from fingertips to elbows
gloved in scales
as if she'd dipped her skin in sequins
and a little blood to make them stick.
Dad sat behind her
nursing his last warm beer,
the only sound the *swhitchh*
of Mother's scraping.

I stood off to one side
inventing what I'd say to them,
wanting so much
a different childhood
and swearing I would never be as unhappy
or alone as they

believing then
I'd keep every single vow I made.

A man and a woman sit near each other.
They have promised God to live together,
they have promised their children
they'll never part. His hands are shaking.
He is trying to move a spoon full of sugar
from the bowl to his cup without spilling any
on the table. She is tearing a Kleenex to pieces
in her lap. How often I have seen them like this,
me sitting in the third chair or not,
the dog under the table waiting for scraps
or perhaps by now the dog is dead. I cut them out
as I used to cut people from the catalogues,
some of them missing an arm or half a leg.
I move them to another place, another table,
a different morning in their lives. Still
they do the same things with their hands, he
tries to move a spoon from the bowl to his cup,
she tears a Kleenex into smaller
and smaller bits.

1

He's five foot eight.
He has a large nose and thick grey hair.
He chews his nails to the quick.

2

He's skinny but he didn't used to be.
His hands and arms were huge from working hard,
from shovelling grain in the elevators for a dollar a
day, from digging sewers for the City with a back-hoe,
from digging trenches in the oil fields. When I was a
kid, he won all the arm-wrestling matches at the Hea-
ley Hotel. I wanted my arms to be as hairy and power-
ful as his.

3

He calls himself Irish and he's proud of it, though he's
third-generation Canadian, his father moving from
Ontario to Saskatchewan, settling on a farm near a
town called Success.

4

He wasn't smart in school, quit in grade eight to help
on the farm. His brains were in his hands, he could fix
anything, his fingers knew exactly what to do.

5

He was famous for two things in the area where he grew up. He was the best driver for miles around Success, could drive to town through any kind of gumbo in his father's Model T. He was the district killer, shot dogs and horses for the neighbours without batting an eye, took pride in that, still likes to tell those stories.

6

He played the fiddle at country dances. Loved Wilf Carter's "Blue Canadian Rockies" and "Strawberry Roan." He married Peggy Ford who loved to dance. She lived across the road on the farm with the big alkali lake where everyone used to swim. He didn't like to swim, didn't like to walk, didn't like to do anything that didn't connect him with a machine. As a kid he even rode his bicycle from the back door to the outhouse.

7

He has flat feet. That's why he lost the farm. He couldn't get in the army so his mother asked him to move to town. That way his younger brother, Orville, would be the only man around and wouldn't get drafted. He and Mom moved into a cook-car abandoned by the railroad in Success, which was already failing, the stores shutting down, the Chinaman moving away. When his mother died she left everything to Orville and Orville kept it all.

8

The Christmas of '41, just after my brother was born, there was no money. He shot a coyote, sold the hide for $5, and bought gifts for everyone. It was the first and last time he spent money on presents.

9

He wasn't there when I was born. He was betting on the horses at the Gull Lake Sports Day. The first time he held me, Mom was mad, he was hungover, his hands shaking.

10

He got throat cancer in 1969, had cigarettes smuggled into the Grey Nun's hospital, smoked a pack of Export A's a day, got well.

11

He caught his right hand in a lawn mower he was repairing, severed the first joints of three fingers. He smashed his left hand between the steel doors of a freight elevator. I was standing beside him. I fainted.

12

He had his gall bladder removed when he was sixty-four. The morning after the operation he pulled out the tubes from his arm and walked to the Legion for a beer.

13

He bought a speedboat when he and Mom were broke. He roared across Duncaren Dam, drunk, in a storm, leaping the waves. The boat finally tipped and he fell in with his clothes and rubber boots on. He can't swim, but he made it to the surface, the boat circling like a shark. Somehow he got in, made it home, didn't tell anyone till years later.

14

He buys hot goods in the bars and sells them for a profit. He cheated his son-in-law when he sold him a car. One time he came home with a rug he bought at an auction sale. When he unrolled it on the living-room linoleum, there was a hole in the middle, big enough to poke your head through. He rolled it up, tied it with a string and took it back, sold it to a Mennonite for twenty dollars more.

15

He collects ballpoint pens with names written on them, like "Ashdown's Hardware," "Ham Motors," "The Venice Cafe." He puts them in the bottom drawer on his side of the dresser. One of them has a drawing of two minks fucking. As a kid I wasn't supposed to know it was there.

16

He never came to the plays I was in, never watched my brother play hockey. He was drunk at my grade twelve graduation (I was the Valedictorian), stayed out the night before and arrived home just as Mom and I were leaving for the gym. He couldn't tie his shoes. Beside the principal at the head table, he fell asleep, his head nodding over the plate of ham, scalloped potatoes, and jellied salad.

17

He uses the word *Bohunk* and the phrase *Jew him down*. One morning out of the blue he told me he'd rather kill me than have me marry a Catholic.

18

He owns the pool tables in the beer parlour at the Legion. Every Saturday morning he cleans the felt and collects his quarters, rolling them in strips of brown paper at the breakfast table. Though he's got cataracts and can't raise his arms above his head (it was all the arm wrestling, my mother says), no one can beat him playing pool. The young guys wait to challenge him after he's had a few beer, but he only gets better. His eyes seem to clear and maybe he forgets how old he is.

19

His favourite breakfast is Cream of Wheat. His favourite supper is roast chicken with mashed potatoes. His favourite bread is store-bought white though Mom bakes her own. His favourite shirt has snap-buttons and two pockets, one for cigarettes, one for pens. His favourite car is an El Camino painted bronze with razor-thin black stripes. Young guys stop him on the street and ask if it's for sale. His favourite story is how he picked up a semi-trailer from the factory in Windsor years ago, drove it through Detroit and all the way to Swift Current without stopping for a sleep. His favourite TV program used to be "Don Messer's Jubilee." He'd always say *Look at old Charlie dance.*

20

He doesn't have a favourite book. The only thing he reads is *The Swift Current Sun.* He follows the lines with the one good finger on his right hand, the nail bitten to the quick, and reads everything three times. I don't know how much he understands.

I want my mother to live forever,
I want her to continue baking bread,
hang the washing on the line, scrub
the floors for the lawyers in our town.
I want her fingers red with cold
or white with water. I want her
out of bed every holiday at six
to stuff the turkey, I want her to cut
the brittle rhubarb into pieces, to can
the crab apples, to grind the leftover roast
for shepherd's pie. I want her to grab me
and shake me out of my boots when I come home
late from school, I want her to lick her fingers
and wipe the dirt from my face. I want her to
put her large breast into my mouth,
I want her to tell me I am pretty, I am sweet,
I am the apple of her eye. I want her to knit and knit
long scarves of wool to wrap us in like
winding sheets all winter through. I want her
to sing with her terrible voice that rose above
the voices in the choir, to sing so loud
my head is full of her. I want her to carry
her weariness like a box of gifts up those stairs
to the room where I wait. Sleep, I will croon
at the edge of her bed, sleep, for tomorrow is
a holiday. Her hands will move in dream, breaking
and breaking bread. Not pain, not sorrow or old age
will make my mother weep. But the sting of onions
she must slice at six a.m., the bird forever
thawing in the kitchen sink, naked and white,
I want so much emptiness
for her to fill.

Just before sunrise
the snow is blue as flax.
Down our street, only one
other house with its windows lit.
Next door the paper boy
climbs the steps, the pompom
on his red tuque bobbing.
Behind him, waiting with his bag
on a wooden sled, a little girl
who could only be his sister,
she looks so proud and happy
to be there. Without his friends around
he doesn't seem to mind,
seems pleased to have her,
the two of them the only ones
on this long blue street
beneath the morning moon.

It could be my brother and me.

How I loved to be with him
even in the cold, even when
he didn't want me there.
I'd sneak out the back
and follow his whistle,
hopping from track to track,
fitting my feet inside his
across the snow.

Finally, his route almost done,
he'd wait for me,
lift me up and put me in his bag

on top of the papers he had left,
carry me home like a kangaroo
nestled in the pouch, warmed
by his body, my eyes barely open,
as if I'd slipped out of him
seven years after he was born,
he, as much as my mother,
giving me this life.

Two days later and I've turned the parade
into a story I tell over drinks. Start with
my favourite part, the band from Cabri,
the whole town marching, children
barely bigger than their horns,
old men and women keeping time. Then,
riding bareback, four Lions' Ladies
in fake leather fringes,
faces streaked with warpaint, not one
real Indian in the whole parade.
Finally the Oilman's Float, a long
flatbed truck with a pumping machine,
a boy holding a sign saying "Future Oilman,"
beside him a girl, the "Future Oilman's wife."
I tell my friends it was as if I'd stumbled
into a movie set in the fifties, that simple
stupid time when everyone was so unaware.

That's my story about the parade,
three parts to the narrative,
a cast of characters, a summing up.
I didn't mention my father
sitting beside me in a wheel chair.
Out of hospital for the day.
My mother putting him in diapers.
In the fifties he wouldn't have been
here beside us but somewhere down the street,
alone and cocky, drunk or about to be.
Or he'd have been racing his speedboat
at Duncaren Dam, the waves
lifting him and banging him down,

a violence he could understand,
that same dumb force raging inside him.
I don't describe my father
in his winter jacket, his legs covered
with a blanket in the hot light
bouncing off the pavement,
the smell of ammonia rising from his lap.

The day after the parade mom called
to say she saw us on TV.
When the camera panned the street
it stopped at us. "Not your dad," she said,
"they just caught the corner of his blanket."
As if he wasn't there.
As if he'd disappeared,
his boat flying through the air,
the engine stalled,
the blades of his propeller
stopped.

He tells my mother
last night he dreamed of dying.
Did you meet anyone you know? she asks.
No, he says. He only made it halfway there.

She is trying not to hold him
back. She unwinds from his hands,
turning her ring three times as she leaves
his room, as if a charm will let him go,
transform the man she knows into a bird
making its way by stars
or a salmon that knows
in its fine articulation of bones
where the stream will lead.

Poor human flesh,
so lost and wandering. Halfway there
a bird will push its small heart
through a cloudy sky, only the Dog Star
breaking through. Impatient, my father
tries to remember what his flesh
must know, the ancient map of stars,
tongues of water speaking
the gravel of his spawning bed.

Mother, knowing he is gone
from the place her body made for him,
wishes she could dream a man
of fins and feathers.
Alone in their double bed,
asleep under stars, she turns
and turns her ring.

One never sees things
the same as another.
Take the Angel of Happiness.
You might see her as a bluebird
and remember the old joke.
Yes, there's that miracle
of colour, that sudden flight,
but there's also birdshit,
meaning everything
has a price.

Myself, I think of my mother
though she hasn't had
a happy life. Still
she carries with her
a certain brightness.
It magnifies the air
the way an angel would
if she walked
through your house,
light falling from her hair.

Today Mom phoned to tell me
she's making a scrapbook,
pulling together pictures
from my childhood.
You were such a pretty girl,
my mother says, so clever
and you never knew it.

This makes me cry
when I get off the phone

though I know she meant well,
wanted me to share her pride
in this child who once was me.
And I do, you know,
somewhere inside I want
to pat that kid on the head,
tell her she did okay
though I wish her life
had been easier.

But mostly I wish that
for my mother. I wish
she'd had more chances
to get her feet off the ground,
to shine with that clarity
I see so often
now she's old.

When she comes to visit
her beauty is right there,
it's moved to the surface
where even she can't deny it
like those miracles
we learned about in Sunday school.
Whatever happened
was tangible and solid,
something everyone, no matter
what they believed,
could see.

What he left me –

an old truck with a big V-8.
I drive it into the country
and stop on this road
far from any house,
turn off the lights.

Sounding the dark

I divide it into things I know:
moths dusting the grass,
the motor clicking
like caraganas pods
as they release their seeds,
an animal – mouse or vole – moving
on soft paws through the milkweed.

And something else, neither
coming nor going nor standing still.

Father, I say out loud
for I have driven here without a map.
I have lost my bearings. *Father*.

Whatever it is that surrounds me
is immense and weightless
and without a name.

It has no need
of wheels or words
or a woman's grieving.

Before the railways were built, what took the place of
stations in people's dreams? JOHN BERGER

Sunday morning, 7 a.m. Already
there are tracks in the snow,
a calligraphy of cats
traced in the alley. Their blue
ideograms read like a Chinese text,
up and down. With a small broom
I sweep the windshield.
I am driving to the station,
meeting a train.

On the platform I want my mother to be there,
as she was, standing with two loaves of bread
in a brown bag, a suitcase with a broken lock
at her feet. I want her to have come
from a different country, to have crossed
all this snow, the train pulling her
into winter and another time.

At the place where she is going
a cat walks across the yard,
placing its back paws precisely
where the front have been.
A man who could be my father
sweeps the steps with an old curling broom,
his name printed on the handle.

By the time he has finished,
the top step is filled with snow.
He sweeps and sweeps

for he knows my mother has no boots.
When she arrives she'll be wearing
a velvet hat, and on her feet
her wedding shoes.

1

Jack. My mother's brother.
The one I never knew.
Grandmother in mid-morning
kneading the bread when she heard
the horses at the gate. Something wrong.
Grandfather tall and stern in the wagon
didn't wait for her as he always did,
but got down himself (*My God, what's wrong?*),
opened the gate,
opened the gate then drove the horses through.
Didn't get down again, didn't loop the wire
over the post, but drove past the barn
up to the house, a small red bundle
beside him in the wagon seat.
Grandmother at the window,
perfectly still,
except for her hands. They twisted
her apron round and round as if they wanted
to tie themselves up, stop her fingers
from tearing out her eyes. (*Don't look!*)
Her boy Jack.
Dead.
Crushed by the wagon wheels.
Giving to the land a son
as if the land demanded it.
The hollow thud of earth
on the wooden box like a cannon shot,
changing forever
the history of the heart.

2

Is there another way to bind us?
(Those small bones
tying the family forever
to the earth.) Not the children
swallowed by the soil, the limbs
eaten by the baler,
the endless grieving of the wind.

Today I saw a farmer in a photograph,
hoisting his body by pulleys
into the combine cab. At his side
a wheel chair, the collapsible kind
you can put into a truck or car.
It sits at the edge of the field
like a detail in a Wyeth painting,
all around the wheat waiting to be cut.

Hands on the wheel, the farmer without legs
is whole again. He walks his combine
in long sure rows all the way
to the horizon and doubles back,
doing what his father did,
looking over his shoulder
at what lies behind,
following
the same straight path across the field
as the land blows away.

3

The word *bucolic.* "Rustic, of the country,"
says the OED: "The shepherds and shepherdesses
milk the cattle, and compose bucolic poems."
Why did the poets lie to us then?
Why did they never speak of the other side:
Uncle Jack, the farmer in the photograph,
the isolate woman who carries water
from the well to her garden that will never grow,
the silence ("O, sweet silence of the golden field")
beautiful if the crop is full
but enough to drive you mad
as you wait for your child
for the first time in her life
to hear the sound of rain. Of *rain.*

The shepherds and shepherdesses after milking,
after shovelling out the barn, after spreading straw,
after hauling hay and water, after feeding, after
mending fences, after separating and scrubbing,
after making butter and cheese, after driving
these to market, after coming home, after milking,
after hauling hay and water...

sit in the fragrant meadows,
                              composing poems.
"O, solitary reaper," they write, "How beautiful
your bowed head among the sheaves of wheat."

4

Or –
Grandmother ran to the gate
when she heard the horses,
ran as she always did, drying her hands
on her apron, Grandfather sitting
tall and imperial on the wagon seat,
the reins of the horses wrapped around
his wrists. And beside him Jack,
the smallest of the boys, the one
who brought laughter into the house
and music, on a tin flute, so my mother says.
Grandmother closed the gate,
closed the gate, Grandfather and Jack
by now at the barn, unhitching the horses
with names like Tony, and Mae and Maude.

Jack was my favourite uncle, O,
he was nimble, he was quick.
He knew the homeplace
as the others didn't,
taking me to see
the fox's den, the small coulee
where herons built their nests,
the buffalo stone. In winter
showing me, the city kid,
what walked before us in the snow.

This was the land to him,
not just what was broken,
the acres the other uncles fought over

when Grandfather died,
but the wild places and the creatures
who lived there, places where
the spirits of the earth,
if they still exist,
might dwell.

5

Grandmother always said
she wanted to be a gypsy.
I never understood
what she meant
when I was a child, could not
see my short, down-to-earth
Grandma who came from Wales
dancing in bracelets
around a fire, selling flowers,
reading palms. (*You will cross
the water. You will bear many children.
You will know hard times.*) Now
when I think of what *gypsy* means,
what people see when they hear
that word, I know
she must have longed
to go somewhere, to be on the road
in a caravan, everything she owned
rolling on wheels.

When a creek dried up,
when the weather or the town turned against you,
you packed up your wagon and drove away

(if you were a gypsy)
and nothing held you to one place.
In the night you were gone.
In the morning you cooked your food
under a sky that made no demands on you.

Strange desire for a woman
who stayed forever on the land
she and Grandpa broke,
a woman who bore seven children,
all moving no farther than the nearest town,

a woman who never danced,
who never had the time (so my mother says)
to grow the roses she loved
or wear their flaming blossoms in her hair.

6

The fox has been poisoned
(to save the chickens in the yard),
the herons were never there
(I remember them from another place)
but the buffalo stone remains
on the hill above the alkali lake
where my mother used to swim,
her skin and hair turning stiff
as if she'd been held by the heels
and dipped in starch.

Not Uncle Jack but she
took me there to her childhood place,

a huge white rock covered with lichens –
crab nebulae exploding
in brilliant orange,
their light reaching us
across a billion years of space. Still
you could see the depression
where the buffalo
rubbed their huge foreheads,
their matted backs,
walking round and round
as if they were turning
a granite wheel
grinding the sky,
the machine of their destruction
bearing down.

Mom showed me
how she used the buffalo stone
for a slide, it was smooth
as glass, and I slid too,
neither of us children then,
but loving this rock
(as it was, as it is,
as it will be) where
the animals gathered.

Below, the hill itself
sliding on wind-slickened grass
into the past,
up to the white-crusted
lips of the silent lake.

7

Nothing can be turned back.
Words cannot change
a life that is past,
make the land whole again
or call the buffalo home.

But what can we glean
from the things that are lost?
Can anything be held
the way a loved one
is held when the body knows
its youth is gone?

Can the past already sown
with its seeds, yield a future
without despair?
Despair for the earth, for those
who live here,
for those who have gone.

8

How I would love to find
the phantom limbs,
lift the child from the earth
and breathe into his open mouth
my song. Tear the boards from
the windows of the house
that bore a family and pushed
each son and daughter like a bird

into the vast, new worlds.
Who will come back to the fields
scraped to the bone, the houses
stripped of paint? The broken
machines, the wells gone dry,
the earth itself giving up,
clouds passing over like the dispossessed,
moving to nowhere
                              we can name
but moving away.

Once by the side of a road
I stopped the car at an empty house
to read what was written there,
No Trespassing,
painted on the weathered boards,
Or You Will Be Shot. Someone Is
Watching You Now.

All I could see was wind
turning the brome grass
like the hands of a clock
round and round in the dust
as if the earth had asked
the wind the time. *Now*

had been written on the wall,
a line of black paint trickling
from the last letter, making me
think of the man who wrote it,
hands that could take apart
and put together

any farm machine,
unskilled
in the making of letters,
the making of signs.

His simple desperate act
to protect what little was left,
the boards he or his father
sawed and nailed,
enclosing in four walls
                    an empty space
within the emptiest space anyone can imagine
outside of the desert or the sea,
stretching so far it makes you think
of eternity, *Someone*
Is Watching You
Now

        9

Where the wire loop
slides over the gate post
there is a depression in the wood,
the grain smooth as satin.

The gate left open.
Nothing leaves
but someone walks through
from then to now,
walks into the yard
and what lies ahead.

Will he close the gate behind him?
Will he leave it open?

What must he atone for
before the land takes him in?

10

My grandparents dead
but the house remains within
the semi-circle of caraganas
Grandpa planted by hand
to break the wind. No matter
how long I look
nothing is written
on the walls, inside or out.

My uncle,
the youngest son who never left,
still lives there in the summers
with his wife, both of them
years older now
than the man who bore the body of a boy
through the gate, the woman who watched.

If my mother were to read this poem,
she'd probably say I'd made too much
of Jack, too much of signs,
the afternoon I spent with her
at the buffalo stone
unreadable
though I finally swam in the lake below,

wanting to feel what she felt
as a child, my skin growing tight,
my mouth closed to the terrible taste
of alkali on my tongue.

For me the farm has always been
her stories. Where I take up the telling,
where I begin and she stops,
I no longer know. There are only
a few things I am sure of
and these I set down here:

It is not the land
that spells the end of things.

From the bones we lay
forever in the earth,
at the urging of sun and wind
something grows,
something rises to the light
and has its say.

My mother had a brother,
Jack.

IV

Moving Toward Speech

The child on the couch,
pretending sleep,
moves toward speech
the way a snail moves,
its soft body
feeling every inch
of the leaf as it climbs,
tasting every scent
moonlight scatters in the air.

His small mouth
curls around the myriad
shapes of sound as he listens
to the hum of conversation in the room.
He knows his mother's voice,
his father's,
but how different they sound
when not speaking to him.

What does he understand
as he hears the vowels,
the hard consonants clicking like peppermints
against his teeth?

He must know the parts
of the body. If his mother says *hand,*
a small bulb glows in his head.
Foot, mouth, nose,
a whole string of lights
flickers across his brain like farmhouses
strung along a road, their windows lit.
If he crosses the yard and climbs the steps

to the wide verandah surely someone
will open the door and let him in.

He finds his way down the road
house by house,
the barking of dogs telling anyone who listens
exactly where he is.

Ahead the city's long luminous
line from east to west
shines like a comet's tail
come down to rest against the earth.

As he gets closer,
the words hook up inside his head
with a loud clang
like the cars of a train, wheels
pulling him forward much too fast

behind him the tall solitary houses,
one by one,
locking their doors,
turning out their lights.

When they built the wall
they had no idea the living would leave
so much stuff underneath the names.
They didn't know the dead had so many
strange requests, didn't know there'd be
so many pilgrims in a country with satellite TV.
The man who cleans up along the wall
can't wait to tell his wife after work each day.
You wouldn't believe what he picks up!
Flowers, letters, photographs, even a Coors,
okay, but a baby carriage full of human hair,
a stuffed alligator, a Lionel electric
train, its cars piled high with wishbones.
They had to build a warehouse to store
everything that piled up, like so much merchandise,
as if the dead still need a shopping mall.
In a ledger each item is carefully described
by a retired bus conductor who used to classify
butterflies in his spare time. He records
the object's height and weight, the exact
place it was found, then lays it on a metal shelf.
He doesn't note its name or use, its possible intent.
One of the painters hired to coat the building
battleship grey, a young man who'd come
from Montana to find his brother's name,
paints the side door lapis lazuli
because he likes the sound of it. He doesn't know
the dead can walk through any kind of blue
as easily as air. At night when all the staff have gone,

when the pilgrims pile in buses, cars and trains,
one after another the dead rattle down the aisles
with grocery carts to claim the one thing
they cannot leave behind: a baseball bat,
a red roller skate, a doll that says *Kiss me, honey,*
when you turn her upside down.

The cancer began in her tonsils,
she'd say it with a smile
almost expecting to be teased
for such a serious disease rooting
in that childish place.
She remembered her son at four
when he'd had his out, the way
he'd looked at her while the nurse
slid the cold thermometer up his bum.
She carried on as usual, cleaned the house,
fried a chicken for her husband
every Sunday, cutting the breast
in four pieces, the wings in two.
The morning of the day she died
she took him down the basement,
showed him how to separate
the clothes, set the dials,
how to hang his shirts and pants
so the creases would fall out.

*

The man with a worn-out heart,
sold his tools so his wife
wouldn't be left with that part of him
to deal with. How he had loved them
in his hands, each so perfectly designed
to fit the palm, the wheels,
bits and teeth made for one specific use.
On the empty walls of the garage
hung the shapes of wrenches, saws and drills.
Years ago he'd traced around them row on row

so he'd know where to hang each one,
know what his neighbour had borrowed
and failed to return. From his pocket
he removed a black felt pen
and in the corner on a board painted white,
he drew the perfect outline of a man.

       *

Before she walked into the river
and didn't come back,
the woman who couldn't remember
the day of the week
or the faces of her children,
made a list of all the men
she'd ever loved,
left it for her husband by the coffee pot,
his name on the bottom,
underlined twice
for emphasis.

The morning cold with dawn,
I stand at the window, first
light spilling through the glass.
Across the yard I see my neighbour
on his front step. He waves,
then points a rifle at my head.

Yesterday he told me
he'd buy a gun to shoot the skunks
who come up from the river,
drawn from the willows to our
apple cores, our overripe
melons and sour milk, our almost
empty jars of jam. Night-raiders,
they dip into the wells
of the garbage cans.

I have imagined them,
their narrow faces
peering in the windows while I sleep,
turning the thin bones of dream
over and over in their paws.

Now it is my neighbour's face
I see through the window,
the precision of his eyes and hands.
He waves and grins, then lines me up,
practises his sight.

We are in this together now.
He studies my face like a lover,
knows the curve of my forehead,

the slight indentation of
my temples, the blue pulse
beating there.

After dark when he waits
in the alley the smell of me
will sting his eyes, fill his mouth,
make his nostrils flare.

For I will have been there
before him,
driving ahead of me
these dark sisters
with their slow walk
down to the river, the white
on their backs blazing
in the moonlight,
their sweet mouths
red with jam.

Bottom-feeders, the sturgeon move
their long snouts through the darkest part
of water, unchanged. Antediluvian
they are older than the oldest man,
older than any spirits of the air.
Grandmother, Grandfather fish,
surely they are holy, worshipped
by the shamans when our world
was full of wonder. Too huge to hold
in the mind, they may be
what we've called Loch Ness, Ogopogo,
fabulous, long-necked monsters
of the lakes, solitary, shy of man.
Along the shores of Lake Superior
when men in the Atlantic walked on cod,
so many sturgeon caught,
they were dragged by teams of horses
from the water's edge, shovelled into furnaces
like the giant trunks of trees
to feed the fire, the oil
in their skin and flesh crackling.
They are a heavy, bony fish
with thick, sucking lips. They are
edible, their eggs consumed as caviar –
black translucent pearls
the female lays after twenty years
without a mate.
              Though they move
where light cannot reach them,
as we move each night in dream,
unchanged, we pull them from
the bottoms of lake or river or sea

without awe or mercy,
thrust them into the sun,
their cold toothless mouths large as caves,
their stunned eyes holding at the last
instant of their ancient lives
a human face.

The bear walks out of the trees with a story. Each one (the bear and the story) bigger than the one before. This time it is night. There is a woman and a small house floating on the snow like a covered sled abandoned by two Percherons who are part of another tale. The woman hears a noise and opens the door, expecting what? Usually it is a man who has walked for miles across the snow as if he's been trudging through a nineteenth-century Russian novel and deserves to be here at the end; a man with a brass cornet covered in frost or a bouquet of roses brittle as glass or a need so large it will lift her off her feet and into the future he has planned. This time there is no man at the door. She opens it and sees nothing. She opens the door and sees nothing but blackness, not even a star, not even the outline of a tree, just the black at the bottom of wells, the black of caves, the black of a scavenger crow that goes for the eyes. She closes the door and wonders what has gone wrong. It is a clear night. The woman who reads the sky knows this is a night full of stars and northern lights, the snowflakes on the ground flickering like fireflies. She opens the door. Utter darkness. But the darkness seems to move, it moves in and out like an animal breathing, like the chest and belly of a grizzly bear. She closes the door. Gently. Now several things could happen. She could grab the gun leaning against the wall and fire into the door, shattering the wood and what is beyond it, but no one would be surprised if she didn't, if the gun wasn't loaded or wasn't there where you'd expect it to be. No one would be surprised to find her crouched in a corner, growing smaller and smaller as she waits once again for the man to come. But this is the bear's story. He never once conjured a gun or a man. He waits for the woman to open the door and embrace the dark. She does more than that. She opens the door and steps right inside his belly, walks into him as if he were the night, becomes part of the story he has carried from the trees, from the cave where he lay sleeping, from his huge and fabulous head.

A heron poises on one leg
in my mind, most still
just before I dream
of flight.

It's the stretching
of his huge wings
that wakens me,
pulls me out of sleep.

I climb from the tent
and put out the fire,
stand in the dark
with only my skin
separating me
from the night.

The stars above me burn
like old scars that shine
because a scalpel
let in light. Nothing
more can hurt me.

The heron's flight
from shore to shore
is a palindrome. It places me
at the beginning at the end.
In the dark alone

I watch the white fires
of the birch

along the lake ignite
as the heron fans his wings
above their branches

so whoever he might be
he can warm himself
as he finds his way
back home.

Moving away from winter, he retires
to the coast, westering, mile zero,

land's end. And what of a garden
I ask? Is there room for that?

Yes, but of a different kind
from the ones he remembers,

the sweet peas his mother planted,
her hands pale spiders in the earth,

the cabbage and potatoes, the anemone
of dill, the rows of beans and beans.

On the coast the soil is thin, a linen
napkin over stones. There, he says,

he'll grow different things, some basil,
a little thyme. He plants the seeds already

in his mind, no fear of frost,
the summer's long, herbs grow

on stony constellations, air
moves in from the sea with its smells

of eternity. Back where he was born
his mother now would be soaking seeds

in a shallow bowl, snow outside the window.
He'd give anything to be there,

crossing time as if it were
a landscape he had dreamed, a garden

large enough to hold desire. She
spreads the packages of seeds

like a deck of cards on the kitchen table,
a royal flush, a winning hand.

She lets him rearrange the rows,
placing peas by broccoli,

carrots by tomatoes, marigolds
along the border. On the coast

he says the names out loud:
Early Bird. Sweet William. Everlasting.

He can see the sun breaking up
the clouds, pools of light

along the window sill, the oilcloth
his mother wipes and wipes,

setting supper plates for people
he'll never see again,

he and she in another time, waiting
for the earth to tilt.

Longing to help you, not
knowing how. Neither of us
says the word out loud
but it lies underneath
everything we speak –
               Oh, what can I do?
Make you supper tonight,
look up a recipe. *Pecan-Breaded*
Chicken Breasts with Mustard Sauce.
Dijon mustard, ground pecans,
vegetable oil, "preferably safflower,"
a tub of sour cream. I will find us
candles, tall and white. At the market
bouquets bound in green paper.
It's January but at least
there are carnations
and in the centre one red rose –
no, not the rose – its bloody petals
(what can I do?) I pad through
the house softly, softly,
smile and smile,
sneak looks at you
over the cover of my book.
Tonight, I say, *I will make us chicken.*
When you come in the door
from the doctor's office
you will smell the oil, smoking.
I won't ask how you are,
(no, not flowers!) I will wait
for you by the stove
and not look up,
  not look up,

brown one side perfectly,
turn each skinned, boned, halved
breaded chicken breast
so carefully in the pan.

He who knew the ways of birds,
the beautiful and common, the thirteen
different shapes of finches' beaks,
ate the meat of jaguar and iguana,
noted in his journals it tasted good.

Among the crew of the *Beagle*
he was known for his sweet temper and his love
of animals. He wrote of the armadillo
he discovered in Brazil:
"It seems almost a pity to kill
such nice little animals, for as
a gaucho said, while sharpening his knife
on the back of one, 'son tan mansos'
(They are so quiet.)" After he had written

the famous book, he sat in his wicker chair
in his country house in Kent,
an obsessive man, numbering
the bees in his garden. He suffered
from nausea, headaches, tension,
paced from room to room
(his seven children and his wife asleep),
and by candlelight as in a boat
sorted through his journals that weighed
two hundred pounds.

All that he had killed,
dissected and shipped in crates to England,
(the Chiloe fox, the jaguarundi,
the quiet armadillo) seemed
to watch him from the study,

his ears ringing with the secrets
of their brains and glands,
their chromosomes
that hadn't been discovered yet,
a diaspora of tongues
so jumbled and unlatinate
he couldn't get them down.

During the day
he walked with his dog along
the edge of the woods on the sandy path
where his children clapped their hands
and called the canine
by its name. He thought of his
colleagues, the vivisectionists,
who severed the vocal chords
of a dog or cat
so it could not scream
as they cut into its flesh. Around him
in his garden the English finches sang.

Between his hours of pencilled notes
his wife, who was his cousin
and whom he had known as a child,
endlessly read him novels
at his request. He demanded
happy endings and heroines
he could love.

Nobody's moon. The crow
with the split tongue
hops through the grass,
searching for his lost feather.

When I call *Who's there?*
he cries *Nobody,* using only one
of his many voices. Nobody
drops a black eye-patch
on my doorstep, a dead
wren on my pillow.
Nobody drags his shadow
like a tired broom across the snow
leaving the trail an animal leaves
when it crawls away from pain.
I am not the one, I say out loud,
the crow calling three times
in his harsh, anonymous voice.

In the middle of my life
I am sitting without anyone,
holding a torn feather
between my fingers. I drag it
across my breasts, my belly,
over my own downy dark.

Out of the sounds I make
comes Nobody, his wings wet
and glistening. As crows do
when they travel on the ground,

he bobs and bobs his head,
saying *yes* to everything
in all his voices.

On the lake two boats riding the storm,
great oars creaking. In one
the milk-smooth heads of the unborn,
their huge eyes reading the clouds
and the absence of light. In the other
the souls of the dead glistening with rain.

At a certain point in the water
the boats cross. Some of the passengers
exchange places, step over the gunwales,
carefully balance, as if they bear
what little weight they carry
on new feet or feet cracked and old,
the boats rocking and rocking in the wind.

See the light they are heading for
across the water. Who is so lonely
as to hang a lamp for them?
Who so foolish, so brave?

What will this person
who waits on the shore
do if they arrive?

There are only so many coats
to keep out the cold,
so many shoes to go around,
so many ribs to hold a heart inside.

Beethoven's arctic hush sitting in his ear,
snow silencing the music as it fell
yet the notes were still there,
ghostly fish beneath a sheen of ice.
Goya heard a ringing in his brain.
It drove him mad, the screech of metal
sawing stone. Perhaps it gave him
the Black Paintings on his farmhouse wall
far from Madrid, his brush
stuttering, the sounds inside
his head forced out into the light.
Dostoevsky banged his heels on the floor,
chewed on a wooden stick, his mouth foaming.
From this came Raskolnikov? Karamazov?
Ilusha and his little boots? An excuse
for pain, an attempt to find meaning in the cells
eating the body from the inside out, the loss
of paradise, the innocent flesh. My mother's
old cliché, *Everything turns out for the best,*
how angry it made me. Everything does not
move toward a perfect end. Not even art
can make it so. In our house on the wall
hangs a painting by a man my age
whom everyone treats as a child,
his nerves tangled, the synapses lost.
We talk to him as if he were deaf,
fill in the awkward pauses in his sentences,
words slippery with drool. At the dinner table
he has trouble getting the fork to his mouth,
his hands are wired, they jerk. Mashed potatoes
fly over his shoulder, splatter the wall.

For us, he has painted dancers in black and white
with wide red sashes. So full of life
they won't stay within the frame but leap
against the glass like bees in a jar.
Sometimes when his hands jump in the air,
swoop and dive above the candle flames,
they are beautiful
like Pavlova far from home
making from her husband's want of love
a dying swan.

It will not know the meaning of
decorous or *Annunciation.*
It will not grace its feet
with embroidered slippers
or wear sensible shoes.
It will not say *rose* as if the word
smelled better than the flower.
It will not hate men –
unconditionally.
It will not be a nursemaid
brought over from abroad.
It will not help you die
the way you think you want to.
It will not split the atom.
It will not split hairs.
It will not save your children
from themselves.
It will not decorate its wrists
with scars or put its head in an oven.
It will not say *vagina.*
It will not teach you how to die.
It will not pay homage to anybody's
mistress.
It will not make it through Security
at the Yellowknife Airport.
It will not forgive.
It will not unlock the mysteries of cats.
It will not save your children.
It will not help you die.

It will bark and growl
and some days it might bite
but always without fail,
it will let you in.

In that city half the people turned into typewriters and the other half into typists. No one had a choice, you just woke up and there you were, one or the other. The ones who underwent the most radical transformation (the typewriters, of course) went to their beds with the others as companions, sweet nurses of keyboards, of the double space, of margins and tabs. Heads on pillows, the typewriters who had lost the art of speaking, opened their mouths and curled back their lips like a dog just before he bites. The typists struck the keys of teeth, their fingers following a pattern the mouths seemed to dictate in a secret language that spoke only to the typists' hands. O what stories those typewriters had to tell! What alphabets of misery rose from the bowels, what veins of laughter, what dictionaries of sorrow spilled from the wombs, the scrotums, what tenderness the eyes had to sing. Even the youngest typewriter, on earth only a few days, had so much tenderness to tell the typists could get no sleep. Faithful to the end, fingers worn, one by one they all dropped dead from exhaustion, no one left but the typewriters lying still and mute in their beds. Mouths hanging open, they dreamed commas, exclamation points, apostrophes, they dreamed enough quotation marks to surround every word ever said.

Because they roll into town on the backs of trucks
with a loud, orange
crash –
tomatoes, apples and melons
moving from the market stalls
to make way for their huge invasion.

Because the grocers pile them row on row
with the same skill that builds stone fences.

Because this fall for the first time, living
as I now do further south, I saw
a whole field, pumpkins tumbling
to the horizon and doubling back,
and I had to stop the car to stare
as if I'd come upon a herd of deer.

Because they are more accurate than calendars or
    clocks.

Because of the grin some mother or father
carves for a child. The nose,
the triangular eyes that look at you
as if they know your face.

Because a candle flickers inside their heads
like memory
striking its paper matches and blowing them out.

Because they are the last
of autumn's light, the last to ripen,

an explosion, a contradiction of
colour in the colourless fields.

Because their flowers are deep yellow,
because their five-lobed leaves resemble hearts,
because *pumpkinseed* is also
the name of a fresh-water
fish resembling perch and the name of a type
of sailing boat.
Because you can therefore travel on a pumpkinseed
across any kind of water, or holding it to your ear,
hear the secrets of the sea.

Because the OED says, "A single pumpkin could
        furnish
a fortnight's pottage."

Because they are not a vegetable
for the delicate, the weak-hearted.
When you knock on their doors, someone
might answer, beckon you inside.

Because they are moons defeated by gravity,

hugging the earth in their orbits, as we do,
dust to dust. Because in soups and pies
and thick slices of pumpkin bread,

we taste what they know of time.

Because of the small distances
they travel on their trailing vines.

Because they float just above the earth
like lighted buoys marking the safest entrance
to the harbour.

Because the deer, born in the spring,
return to the pumpkin fields
after the harvest
and are lost,
though they nibble with their soft mouths
the broken shells left on the ground
and slowly
find their way.

Because the first snow falls,
the first snow falls,
into the huge silence
the pumpkins leave
in the fields.

> Animals created by silence came forward from
> the clear/and relaxed forests where their lairs were.
> RILKE (translated by Robert Bly)

They come forward now
on moon-bright hooves,
on four perfect paws.

No one is looking for them any more.
The world is a new place.

Wind pauses in the cattails,
holds its tongue. Under the ice,
the mounds of leaves, the mouths
of the traps have all been sprung,
their one word snapped in two.

One by one
they come from their lairs.
Beautiful, immense,
they lie in the clear,
they sleep in the sun. Now
there is only the snow

the snow and the silent animals
free in the forest,
the luminous meadows,
with no one
to call their names,
no one to name them.

The drumming of the moth
on the chimney glass
draws the soldiers from the fields
where they lie like cut wheat,
what is left of their jackets
wet with rain. Their hats
have fallen, their boots
no longer fit. Leather boats
whose seams have split
they sink into the earth
as if it were the sea,
yet the young men rise,
move to the measure of wings.

So small they have become,
so pale and thinly drawn,
no one sees them as they pass.
Not the farmer pitching hay,
the sinews in his arms thick as rope.
Not his daughter who whistles
for her pony at the gate.

As they march, one of them plays
a flute fashioned out of bone,
a sound the girl mistakes
for the blackbird's trill,
its three warning notes
quickening the air.

Whenever she hears it
she wants to go somewhere,
leave her father and her pony

at the gate, find a place
where no one knows her name.
Right now if someone stopped
and touched her,
her whole body would start to sing.

The moth beats on the glass
softly as the heartbeats
of a bird wrapped in wool.
Such a sad sound, this
faint, dusty drumming,
heard only by the smallest,
the most invisible of ears.

After the land has turned to salt,
after the geese die of cholera,
the lambs of suffocation,
after the men have gone
with their machines and chemicals
and the fields lie deserted and nothing grows,
the old women so long forgotten
even dreams can't find them,
come from the places memory can't reach.

They open the doors of the boarded-up houses
and follow the wind to the fields.
They take off their soiled aprons,
their dresses, their underclothes
and let them fly, the wind filling the sky
with the shape of them, their smell
of the earth and the animals
that live beneath it.

The old women naked at last and out in the wind
move in a circle, their feet
never leaving the ground.
They sing to the earth of their dried-up breasts,
their old women's bellies,
they sing their sour breath,
the hour of their birth and their bloody birthings.

When the land is whole again,
their hair will grow
from the mouths of the crocus,
their bones break through the soil
like the knuckles of a giant fist.

And the wind will carry the sound of them,
the words they sang in the sere white fields
when no one was there to hear them,
the alkali eating their tongues.

The consolation of horses
in the meadow, yes, you console
though rarely am I near you.
You come to the fence (truth is
I almost fear you) out of fog or snow,
stretching long chestnut throats
for oats rattled in the pail,
grass pulled by the handfuls,
and sometimes you come only for the word *horse*
sung in the ear, first nominative and last
in the vast, ungulate kingdom
where the eye is more beautiful
because horses have walked through it.

In the stalls of the barn
hung with hoarfrost, harnesses and bells,
your breath so tall above me
is a small consolation.
And when I ride the wide arc of your ribs
as I did as a child on a dappled, creamy mare
whose big bleached bones
now dazzle the meadow, you
find the latent heart of
wood, grass and stone,
hoof by thudding hoof.
For you everything is movement,
everything is sound.

When you lower your great head,
graze so close to the ground,
you hear what lies beneath it,

the grey horses of the dead
moving from one darkness to another,
hoofbeats soft and slow
as though they walked on snow
without falling through.

APR - - 2010